HOW IT WORKS
GASOLINE ENGINES

by Pam Watts

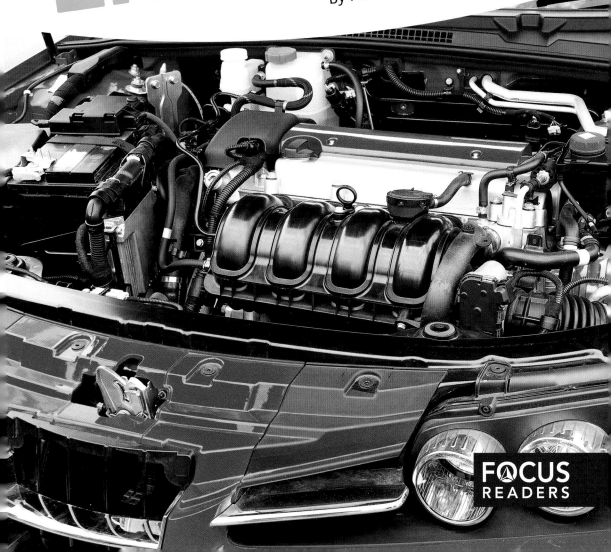

FOCUS READERS

WWW.FOCUSREADERS.COM

Focus Readers is distributed by North Star Editions:
sales@northstareditions.com | 888-417-0195

Produced for Focus Readers by Red Line Editorial.

Content Consultant: Jeffrey Cook, Adjunct Professor, Electrical and Computer Engineering Department, University of Michigan

Photographs ©: Lena Pan/Shutterstock Images, cover, 1; Blanscape/Shutterstock Images, 4–5; Morphart Creation/Shutterstock Images, 7; Dmitry Eagle Orlov/Shutterstock Images, 8; carlofranco/iStockphoto, 10–11; Toa55/iStockphoto, 12; choja/iStockphoto, 14; Artwork Studio BKK/Shutterstock Images, 15; aydinmutlu/iStockphoto, 16–17; Vasyl S/Shutterstock Images, 19; Vectorworks Enterprise/Shutterstock Images, 21; asharkyu/Shutterstock Images, 22–23; Raisman/Shutterstock Images, 24–25; smontgom65/iStockphoto, 26; dreamnikon/iStockphoto, 28

ISBN
978-1-63517-234-8 (hardcover)
978-1-63517-299-7 (paperback)
978-1-63517-429-8 (ebook pdf)
978-1-63517-364-2 (hosted ebook)

Library of Congress Control Number: 2017935882

Printed in the United States of America
Mankato, MN
June, 2017

ABOUT THE AUTHOR

Pam Watts is a writer and educator in the San Francisco Bay Area. She holds a BA in Physics from Wellesley College and an MFA in Writing for Children from Vermont College of Fine Arts. She has written three other children's science books, and her essays have appeared in *Teaching Tolerance* and *Odyssey Magazine*.

TABLE OF CONTENTS

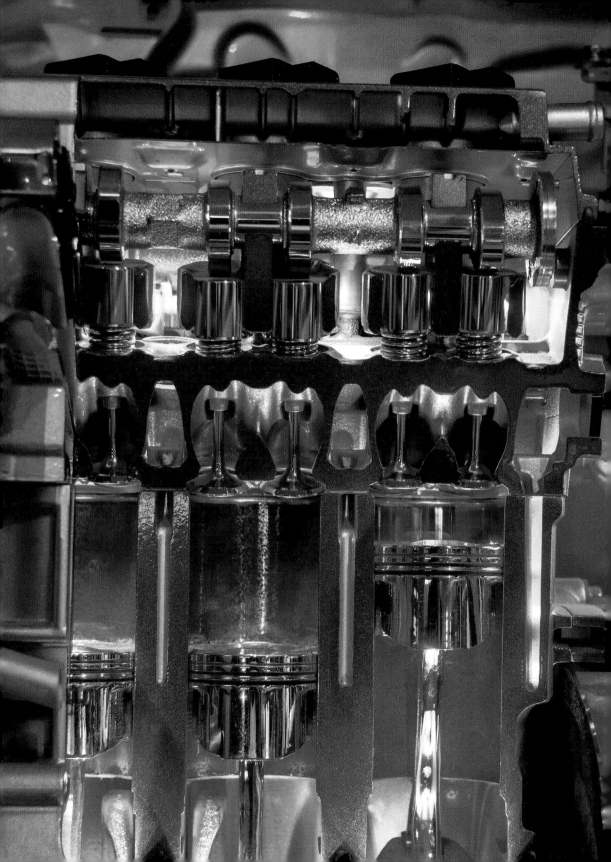

CHAPTER 1

PRODUCING POWER

In the 19th century, people often traveled in horse-drawn carriages. But they had to stop when their horses got tired. Plus, they could only carry as much as their horses could pull. Many people wanted to travel faster and farther. Inventors worked to create carriages moved by engines instead of horses.

An engine's moving parts produce power.

The engines needed power to run. Three main power sources were possible. One possibility was electricity. By 1900, a company in New York City operated an entire fleet of electric taxis. These taxis got power from batteries.

Most places, however, did not have electricity yet. Charging the batteries was not practical. Inventors looked for other fuel sources.

Some engines used steam instead. Steam engines used common fuels such as kerosene and gasoline. These fuels were burned in a boiler. The boiler heated water and made steam, which was used to

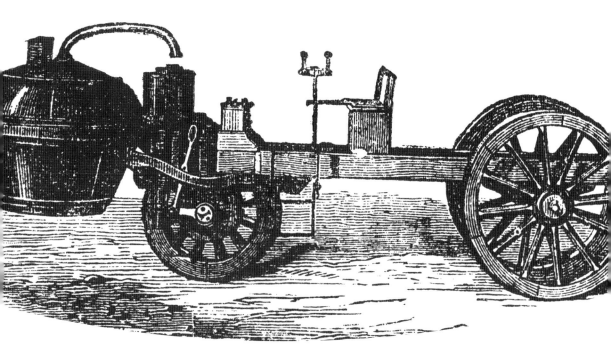

Some early vehicles, such as this tricycle from 1770, got power from steam.

generate power. But the technology was tricky to get right. It never caught on.

The third power source was **internal combustion** fueled by gasoline. By 1876, Nikolaus Otto designed a basic gasoline engine. It was a four-stroke internal combustion engine.

German inventor Gustav Schuermann developed another version of the four-stroke engine in 1888.

Unlike earlier gasoline engines, Otto's engine **compressed** a mixture of gas and air before burning it.

The gasoline engine became the engine commonly used in cars. It also had other benefits. Until the 1930s, many rural areas in the United States did not have electricity. These areas used gasoline engines to generate power. The engines could run washing machines or generators. This made doing other jobs easier, too.

Otto's basic design is still used in most cars today. But the gasoline engine has improved in many ways since then. Today, it is more efficient and more powerful. It is also lighter, quieter, and cleaner.

CRITICAL THINKING

What are some benefits that could result from gasoline engines being lighter, quieter, and cleaner?

CHAPTER 2

IT STARTS WITH A BANG

Engines use **energy** from fuel to do **work**, such as moving a car forward. Burning fuel releases the energy. In most car engines, a piston does the work. It moves up and down inside a cylinder. The piston makes four motions. Each motion is called a stroke. The four strokes form a cycle.

Most car engines have more than one cylinder.

 Mechanics help keep a car's engine running smoothly.

The first stroke is called the intake stroke. During this stroke, the piston starts at the top of the cylinder. It moves to the bottom of the cylinder. Gasoline must be combined with air to burn. So while the piston moves, the intake **valve** opens. As the piston moves down, it creates a partial **vacuum**. Air is pulled into the cylinder through the intake valve.

At the same time, a fuel injector sends fuel into the cylinder.

The second stroke is the compression stroke. During this stroke, the intake valve closes. The piston moves from the bottom of the cylinder back to the top. As it moves, the piston squeezes the fuel and air in the cylinder into a smaller space. This raises the mixture's pressure and temperature. A spark plug at the top of the cylinder creates a spark. It causes the air and fuel to explode. This releases energy. It also creates high pressure at the top of the piston.

When the air and fuel explode, the high pressure pushes the piston back down.

Engine oil helps all the parts of an engine slide together smoothly.

This is the third stroke. It is sometimes called the power stroke. During the power stroke, the work from the engine is sent through the crankshaft to the car's wheels. The crankshaft is connected to the piston. It changes the up-and-down motion of the piston into rotating motion. This causes the car's wheels to turn.

The last stroke in the cycle is the exhaust stroke. During this stroke, the piston moves back up to the top of the cylinder. While the piston moves, another valve called the exhaust valve opens. The piston pushes the burned gas out this valve and into the car's exhaust pipe. At the end of the exhaust stroke, the exhaust valve closes. The intake valve opens, and the cycle starts over.

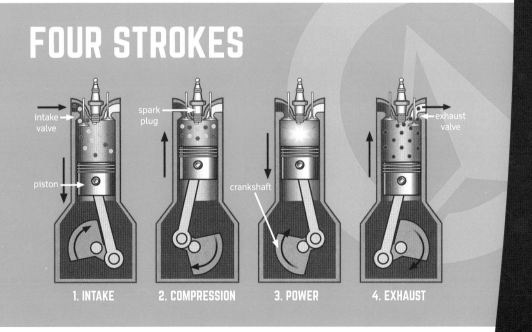

FOUR STROKES

intake valve

spark plug

exhaust valve

piston

crankshaft

1. INTAKE

2. COMPRESSION

3. POWER

4. EXHAUST

CHAPTER 3

PART OF A SYSTEM

Several other parts help the engine with combustion. The fuel tank holds the gasoline that the engine needs. The battery supplies energy to start the engine. Very old cars did not have electric starters. People had to use a hand crank connected to the crankshaft to get the engine started.

A car's fuel tank holds the gasoline.

The **transmission** sends power from the engine to the driveshaft. The driveshaft turns the car's wheels. The transmission controls how fast the driveshaft turns. It also makes sure the right amount of **torque** goes from the engine to the wheels.

A camshaft makes sure the intake and exhaust valves open and close at the right times. As the camshaft rotates, curved parts called cams push down on the valves. This causes the valves to open.

The engine control unit (ECU) controls the fuel injection and spark plug. The ECU is a computer that makes sure the engine runs well. It collects information from

A timing chain connects the crankshaft and camshaft.

sensors on the camshaft and crankshaft. The ECU uses this information to calculate exactly when to inject fuel and fire the spark plug. Other sensors measure how much air goes into the engine and how much oxygen is in the exhaust. The ECU uses that information to inject the right amount of gasoline.

This gives the engine the cleanest, most efficient combustion. The ECU also checks for problems with the engine.

Combustion generates a lot of heat. Too much heat can damage the engine. For this reason, a car usually has a radiator near the engine. The radiator keeps the engine cool.

After air and fuel are burned in a car's engine, the leftover gases contain harmful chemicals. An exhaust pipe sends these gases out of the car. In most modern cars, the exhaust passes through a muffler. The muffler quiets the noise of the explosions inside the engine.

The exhaust also passes through a catalytic converter. This part changes almost all the chemicals into water and less-harmful gases such as nitrogen and carbon dioxide.

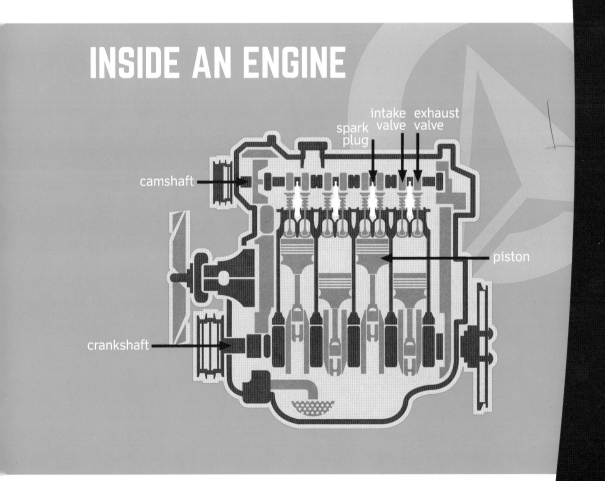

INSIDE AN ENGINE

spark plug

intake valve

exhaust valve

camshaft

piston

crankshaft

THE TRANSMISSION

The transmission helps a car's wheels turn at the proper speed. It also helps them turn with enough torque to move the car. It uses a series of gears. The gears are locked together and forced to rotate together. The gears have different numbers of teeth. A gear with 20 teeth takes longer to turn than a gear with 10 teeth. The ratio between the teeth of two gears is called the gear ratio. This ratio allows the high speed of the engine to be converted into lower speed for the wheels.

The transmission can change which gears are used. Lower gears have higher gear ratios. If a car is in low gear, the wheels will turn more slowly. But they will turn with higher torque. The car can drive up steep hills or pull heavy loads.

The gears in a car's transmission are inside the gearbox.

CHAPTER 4

THE FUTURE OF FUEL

There are more than one billion motor vehicles on the roads today. Most of them use gasoline engines. Modern gasoline engines produce much less **pollution** than early gasoline engines. They also use less fuel to generate more power. But their exhaust still contains some harmful chemicals.

Checking a car's engine regularly helps owners identify problems.

 Cars with only electric motors must be plugged in at charging stations to get power.

Engineers are working to make engines cleaner and more efficient. A turbocharger increases an engine's power. Small turbocharged engines can produce as much power as larger standard engines. Variable camshaft timing can increase power, too. It also reduces the combustion temperature. As a result, less harmful gases are formed. Both of these methods help engines have better fuel economy and lower **emissions**.

Some engineers are returning to an old idea. They are designing vehicles that use electric motors. Electric motors do not create any exhaust. In many cases, this would help reduce pollution.

Some hybrids can use their battery to drive up to 35 miles (56 km) before switching to using the gasoline engine.

However, the electricity to run these vehicles comes from power plants. Many power plants burn coal to generate electricity. The pollution from these power plants might be worse than the exhaust from gasoline engines.

Hybrid vehicles have both an electric motor and a gasoline engine. Hybrids combine power from the motor with power from the engine. This allows hybrid cars to have smaller engines that use less gasoline. Sometimes hybrids can run using electricity alone. When the electricity runs out, they can run like gasoline-powered cars. As of 2017, there were more than 11 million hybrids on the road.

CRITICAL THINKING

What other kinds of fuels might be used to power car engines?

FOCUS ON
GASOLINE ENGINES

Write your answers on a separate piece of paper.

1. Write a paragraph that summarizes the current problems with gasoline engines and the work scientists are doing to solve those problems.

2. Would you want to own a hybrid car? Why or why not?

3. How many strokes does a typical car's engine have?

    A. four
    B. six
    C. eight

4. What would happen if an engine's intake valve did not open?

    A. The driver could not add gasoline to the fuel tank.
    B. The fuel injector could not send gasoline into the cylinder.
    C. Air could not enter the cylinder.

Answer key on page 32.

GLOSSARY

compressed
Pressed or squeezed to fit into a smaller space.

emissions
Chemicals or substances that are released into the air.

energy
The ability to do work.

internal combustion
Burning air and fuel inside an engine to generate power.

pollution
Harmful substances that collect in the air, water, or soil.

torque
A twisting force that causes an object to rotate.

transmission
A set of gears that send power from the car's engine to the wheels.

vacuum
An empty space where there is no air or other gas.

valve
A device that opens and closes to control the flow of a liquid or gas.

work
When force moves an object over a distance.

TO LEARN MORE

BOOKS

Eboch, M. M. *The 12 Biggest Breakthroughs in Transportation Technology*. Mankato, MN: 12-Story Library, 2015.

Kenney, Karen Latchana. *Shop Tech: The Science of Cars*. Mankato, MN: Compass Point Books, 2011.

Petersen, Christine. *Inventing the Hybrid Car*. Mankato, MN: The Child's World, 2016.

NOTE TO EDUCATORS

Visit **www.focusreaders.com** to find lesson plans, activities, links, and other resources related to this title.

INDEX

Answer Key: 1. Answers will vary; **2.** Answers will vary; **3.** A; **4.** C